Benefits of Whipsaws
In
Can't Lose Stock Trades

By Edward Ngureco

Copyright

Risk Disclosure

This document is about trading in the stock market and as such readers are asked to take note of the risk disclosure stated below:

1. Past performance of a stock trading method is not indicative of future results.

2. Past performance of a stock or any equity does not guarantee future results.

3. Trading stocks carries a high level of risk, and may not be suitable for all investors.

4. Trading stocks can result in you losing some or all of your initial investment.

5. You should not trade stocks in money you can not afford to lose.

6. The contents of this document are not a solicitation to buy or sell any financial market.

7. The contents of this document are for general information and educational purposes only.

8. Before trading in stocks, seek advice from your stock broker or an independent financial advisor.

9. Consult your tax advisor for tax consequences on short term profits or losses on trading stocks.

10. Hypothetical performance results have many inherent limitations.

Table of Contents

I. Introduction

Any person who intends to make a living from trading the stock market needs a trading strategy which will reliably gives consistent profits. I have attempted to provide in these pages a profitable trading strategy drawn from my own experience. It's my belief that experience is the best teacher.

The mention of the phrase 'can't lose stock trades' should make many people raise eyebrows, and with a good reason. This is because many of us have spent several years juggling on how to trade stocks successfully but all in vain. When we buy a stock hoping the price will continue heading in the current direction, the current price direction may immediately move in the opposite direction as soon as we have bought the stocks. These up and down movements of the stock prices are called whipsaws. Whipsaws are nuisance to stock traders. They are frustrating and many people will surrender their trades giving the market a chance to take money out of their stocks. Whipsaws, like medicine, can be disastrous to your trades and can also be a cure to your trades, if well utilized.

If you look around, you will see isolated cases of people who seem to know how to make money from the stock market. There must be some things these people do know that others don't. Historically, the stock market has over the time been proven to be a wealth builder to those who understands it. Ideally, the stock market should benefit all those who buy stocks - it's only fair that each one of us, regardless of one's status, be entitled to a piece of the action. Unfortunately that is not the case because in real sense, millions of people are losing their hard earned money to the stock market whilst a few men and women are making huge profits consistently.

There are hundreds of stock trading strategies out there and each has its own story to tell. This document will not dwell on them but will assume the reader has a basic understanding about them, or can easily get access to that information. The statement, 'can't lose stock trades', is indeed a very strong statement, and this document will try to qualify how to set up such stock trades. It is hoped that you as the reader will appreciate the logic behind 'can't lose stock trades' and if not, then, there is no much I can help you with.

II. Getting Started

1. Why Buy Stocks?

People buy stocks or shares in a company in anticipation that the company will grow. Correspondingly, their investments in the stocks will grow as well and pay them dividends. When you buy shares of a company, you become a part owner of the company in proportion to the number of shares you own. In general, people buy shares of a company for the following reasons:

1. As an investment in anticipation the company will grow and prices of the shares will increase.

2. To become part owner of the company with voting rights during annual stockholders meetings.

3. To be entitled to receive dividend payments.

4. To speculate in anticipation that the price will increase and sell the shares at a profit.

5. For pride – some people may feels great when they hold thousands of shares in company XYZ even if a single share has a market value of $0.001.

The bad thing about common stocks is this: if the company goes under liquidation, preference shares, debts and lawyers are paid first. Whatever remains, if any, is what is shared proportionally between the common stockholders.

The truth is, and this is debatable, a stock is nothing if it's not making you money. Throw it away by selling it to the nearest stockbroker and invest the proceeds to something else.

2. Holding Stocks in Street Name

In the olden days, when investors bought stocks they had to take physical possession of share certificates under their names. In today's electronic age, only a small percentage of investors are holding their actual stock certificates. Instead, most stocks are today held by stock brokers under 'street name'. What this means is that when you buy a stock it will be under the name of your stock broker. Your stock broker will have provided you with an account where you can monitor the current net liquidation value of your stocks, reports of stock splits, dividends earnings, annual reports, as well as the ability to sell your shares direct from the account. Your proof of ownership is in the form of a statement that is mailed to you by your broker every month. By holding the stocks under street name, the stockbroker is able to track all stocks electronically facilitating instant sale if a client desires to do so.

When your stocks are held in a street name, the company that issued the shares is not aware that you own the stocks. What they know is that your shares are owned by your stock broker as it's their name that shows in the company's register.

It's safe to have your shares held by your broker and it's the way to go. Like banks, a brokerage firm can go bankrupt. Fortunately, the law requires all brokerage firms be insured with Securities Investor Protection Corporation (SIPC). In the event a brokerage firm goes bankrupt, SIPC will take over and compensate the customers with cash and refund the securities that the brokerage firm held. What you may be compensated has a maximum ceiling and it's advisable to check this out from SIPC. Compensation can also take a minimum of three months.

3. Choosing a Good Stockbroker

Different stock traders have different needs when it comes to choosing the right stockbroker. Help and customer support is considered to be very important by many stock traders. This may be true for the first three months of trading. Thereafter, the customer will have learnt much of what is required in the chosen brokerage firm and may not need much of their help and support. If you plan to be a frequent trader of stocks, the most important feature to consider when choosing a stockbroker should be fees and commissions. If you get it wrong in choosing a broker with lower fees and commissions at the beginning, then, be prepared to pay that extra charge for a very long period in as long as you trade using that broker. This can add up to be a lot of money in the long run. High brokerage commissions can also prevent you do combinational trades that you may want to do, this is especially true for the complex trading strategies that involves stock options.

In your search for stockbrokers who has workable stock trading commissions, you may have to consider these two examples:

1. Stockbroker 'A' charges a commission of $0.01 per share. This means you pay $0.1

for 10 shares, $1.0 for 100 shares and $10.0 for 1000 shares.

2. Stockbroker 'B' charges a commission of $9 for 1000 shares or less. This means you pay $9 for 10 shares, $9 for 100 shares and $9 for 1000 shares.

Stockbroker 'B' is cheaper than stockbroker 'A' for trading 1000 shares. Stockbroker 'A' is cheaper than stockbroker 'B' when you trade less than 1000 shares. Stockbroker 'B' is very punitive for those trading small lots of shares and should be avoided unless you are a large trader who does not envisage yourself trading less than 1000 shares at any one given trade. Stockbroker 'A' is very transparent and is indeed giving you sufficient leeway to be flexible in your trading strategies.

There are many characteristics that you should consider when determining who to choose as your stockbrokers. You may want to consider, among others features, the following characteristics:

1. Sound financial standing

2. Fees and commissions - on stocks and options per share/contract

3. Minimum account opening balance

4. Data subscription fee

5. Margin rates

6. Account maintenance fee

7. Trades offered – stocks, options, exchange traded funds

8. Ease of use of the trading platform

9. Mobile trading tools

10. Fees for virtual trading accounts

11. Help and customer support

12. Other types of investments offered

13. Minimum shares you can buy in one order

14. Will they allow you to short stocks

There are hundreds of stockbrokers out there that one can chose from. What follows below are a few online brokers (listed in no particular order) that one can investigate and find out if they are suitable for your stock trading needs:

1. Interactive Brokers

2. Charles Schwab

3. TD Waterhouse

4. E*TRADE

5. Fidelity

6. Scottrade

7. Ameritrade

8. Firstrade

9. Vanguard

10. Wang Investment

11. Trading Direct

12. OptionsXpress

13. Lowtrades

14. ChoiceTrade

15. MB Trading, etc., etc.

4. Types of Brokerage Accounts

Before you start trading in stocks, you will need to open a brokerage trading account with a stock broker. There are many types of accounts that one can open with a stockbroker. The account you open will depend on the level of service you need from your stockbroker. The most common brokerage accounts are:

1. Cash account
2. Margin account
3. Discretionary account

For the scope of this document, we are only interested in the first two accounts - cash account and margin account.

4.1. Cash Account

Once you have funded your cash account with the minimum opening balance, your broker should allow you to go ahead and use your funds to buy stocks. Now that you have purchased your stocks, you can hold them for as long as you may want without caring much. There is a stock trading strategy that uses the logic that if you buy stocks, holds them for a long period of time. You should only sell your stocks only at a price higher than what you initially paid for them. A cash account is very good for 'buy and hold' trades. But there are also some drawbacks in a cash account. In a cash account, if you sell your stocks, you are required to wait for three days for the trades to 'settle' before you can use the proceeds - perhaps to buy more stocks. In a cash account, you may not 'short' stocks. In a cash account, you may not trade in stock options.

4.2. Margin Account

The other type of account that is popular with many stock traders is the margin account. In a margin account you pay only 50% of the cost of buying stocks and the remaining 50% balance is automatically loaned to you by your broker. As an example: if you have $5,000 in your account, you can buy 1,000 shares of stock XYZ at $10 for a total cost of $10,000. Your cash contribution in this will be $5,000 (50%) and your broker will loan you $5,000 (50%). Having loaned you 50% of the money required to buy the stocks, your broker will then require you to maintain a 'minimum maintenance margin of say 30%. This minimum maintenance margin will vary from broker to broker but usually not less than 25%. If the price of XYZ stock now falls to $7, your 1,000 shares will now be worth $7,000. Your broker had loaned you $5,000 which will represent 71% of the net liquidation value of your 1,000 shares. At this time your money in the stocks will be representing only 29% of the value of the 1,000 shares. 29% is below the minimum maintenance margin your broker allows and he will issue you with a margin 'call'. You will now be required to add cash or equity in your account so that your money in those 1,000 shares is always above the minimum maintenance margin of 30%. If you do not send more cash or equity, then, your broker will sell some or all your shares. As you can see, you may have wanted to hold your stocks for a long period of time so that they can achieve the best returns, but a margin account may not always allow you to do that.

On the other hand, if the price of your stock XYZ was to increase to $20, your 1,000 shares will be worth $20,000 up from $10,000 (at this point your input is worth $15,000). But your broker will always want to provide a minimum 50% of the value of your stocks as a loan. In this case it's a loan of $10,000 from your broker and $10,000 (50%) from yourself. In an investment that cost $10,000 to setup and now that your broker is providing $10,000 in that investment, it means that all your initial contribution of $5,000 cash will be credited back in your account. This $5000 is now free for you to use in buying more stocks or withdraw for personal use. As you can see, you now own 1,000 shares of stock XYZ and your initial money is intact in your account - this is the beauty of a margin account.

5. Short Selling of Stocks

Short selling of stocks is the selling of stocks that you do not own. You borrow the stocks from your stock broker and you sell them at the current market price. This is done when you think the price of the stocks will go down and that in a future date you will be able to buy the shares at a lower price in the stock market. In future, you will have to buy the stocks at whatever price so that you can deliver them back to your stock broker. Shorting of stocks works like this: You feel that the price of the stock XYZ at $20 will decrease in the near future. You borrow 1000 shares of XYZ from your broker and you sell the borrowed shares at $20 each which will give you a cash of $20,000. That cash will be in your account but held by your broker in such a way that you can not use it. In addition, your broker will require you to provide an extra, say, 50% collateral in form of cash or equity. Three weeks down the line the stock XYZ price has dropped to $10. You buy 1000 shares of stock XYZ at $10 for a total cost of $10,000. You refund the 1,000 shares of XYZ to your stock broker and he releases back to you $20,000 which you had initially gotten when you sold the 1,000 shares of stock XYZ. Your profit will be $20,000 – $10,000 equals to $10,000.

If the price of stock XYZ was to rise to a price of $30, then you would have to buy it for $30,000 so that you can refund it back to your stock broker. In this case you will make $20,000 less $30,000 equals a loss of $10,000.

We have already said that most stocks are held by brokers under street name. This would rightly suggest that brokers have lots of shares they are willing to lend out to short sellers. When you opt in for a margin account, you are in essence giving your stockbroker the mandate to lease out your stocks if need arises. When your stocks are leased out for short selling and on the process they pay dividends, you are paid 'payments in lieu of dividends' instead of receiving real dividends. It's also true that you as the owner of the stocks can lose voting rights during that period your stocks are leased out. But on a positive side, you may earn yourself a small interest from the lease of your stocks.

Sometimes, there can be scarcity of stocks to short. This scarcity can lead to a higher interest rate to have the shares for short selling. The process of shorting stocks may seem time consuming but it will take your stock broker just a moment to complete the process, just as it would take them when you want to buy stocks.

The beauty of a margin account is that you can easily trade the stocks on the uptrend as well as on the downtrend. You buy the stock 'long' for the uptrend trading and you short sell the stock for the downtrend trading.

6. Types of Stock Orders

If you want to buy or sell a stock, you will need to place an order with your stock broker. Usually this is done through a standalone trading platform provided to you by your broker. You will need to download and install their software in to your computer. With the advancement of mobile devices, stock orders can also be placed through a cell phone that is internet enabled.

When you buy a stock, you are actually going 'long' that stock. When you sell a stock you don't own, you are actually going 'short' that stock. When you want to buy 100 shares of stock XYZ, you will tell your broker, "buy to open 100 XYZ" shares. When that order is filled, you are now "long 100 XYZ" shares. After a few days you may want to sell your 100 XYZ shares. You will tell your broker, "sell to close 100 XYZ" shares.

When you sell a stock that you do not own, you are actually shorting that stock. When you want to sell 200 shares of stock XYZ that you do not own, you will tell your broker, "sell to open 200 XYZ" shares. When that order is filled, you are now short

200 XYZ shares. After a few days you may want to buy your 200 XYZ shares to cover your short positions. You will tell your broker "buy to close 200 XYZ" shares.

To short a stock, you will need collateral or a margin of about 50% market value of the stock plus the proceeds of the sale of the stock will be retained by your broker. Under Regulation T, the Federal Reserve Board requires all short sale accounts to have the full value of the short sale proceeds (100%), plus an additional margin requirement of 50% of the value of the short sale.

There are different types of stock orders that have been developed over the time. Different types of stock orders are developed to meet specific needs of stock traders. These needs include limiting risk, fast execution, price improvement, use of discretion as well as proper timing. A few of the most common order types includes the following:

1. Market order – This is an order to buy or sell a stock at the bid price or offer price that is currently available in the market. Market order is the most basic type of stock order. A market order ensures your order has to get filled at the current market price. It may happen that when the market is moving very fast, the market order can sometimes get you a price far away than expected. If you want to buy 100 shares of XYZ, you will tell your broker "buy to open 100 XYZ at market".

2. Limit Order – This is an order to buy or sell a stock at a price you specify or better. A limit order is one of the most secure order types as it ensures your order get filled at least at the price you specify.

The bad thing about limit order is that whilst you wait for price to be reached, the market may go in the opposite direction and you order may never get filled at that price you believed is right. If want to buy 100 shares of XYZ at $10.05, you tell your broker "buy to open 100 XYZ at limit $10.05".

3. Stop Market Order – This is an order to buy or sell a stock at market order once the specified stop price is attained or penetrated. A stop order is not guaranteed of a specific execution price. A stop market order is mostly used in stop loss orders. A stop market order can give you results that are far from expectations especially when the markets gap up/down significantly at the open and trigger your stop market order.

4. Stop Limit Order - A stop limit order will become a limit order once the specified stop price is reached or penetrated.

5. A Discretionary Order is a limit order where you will define a discretionary amount, which is added to or subtracted from the limit price, that increases the price range over which the order is eligible to execute. The original limit price is displayed to the market.

6. Trailing Stop Order - A trailing stop for a sell order sets the stop price at a fixed amount below the market price. If the market price rises, the stop loss price rises by this amount, but if the stock price falls, the stop loss price remains the same. A trailing stop for a buy order sets the stop price at a fixed amount above the market price. If the market price falls, the stop loss price falls by this amount, but if

the stock price rises, the stop loss price remains the same.

7. Conditional Order - a conditional order is an order that will automatically be submitted or cancelled only if specified criteria for one or more defined contracts are met. As an example, you can say this: Buy to open 100 XYZ if NASDAQ Index goes below 2000.

Time in Force for Stock Orders: The time in force for a stock order defines the length of time over which the stock order will continue being active before it is canceled. Time in force can be 'Day' or can be 'Good-Til-Cancelled'.

8. DAY - A Day Order expires at the close of the trading day if it does not execute in the course of the day. Unless you specify otherwise, every order should default to a Day order.

9. Good-Til-Canceled (GTC) - A Good-Til-Canceled order will continue to work in the marketplace until it executes or is canceled by the trader. GTC is used on Limit, Stop, and Stop-Limit orders. You should keep an eye on your GTC orders as sometimes GTC orders may be cancelled under certain conditions - for example, GTC orders can be cancelled when a corporate action is taken on a company's stock , or when you do not log in to your account for, say, three months.

10. Bid Ask Spread: In the stock market, just like any other market, the price of a stock will display the bid price as well as the ask price. The bid price is lower than the ask price. The bid price is the price the buyers are willing to pay for the stock. The ask price is the price the sellers are willing to sell the

stock. The difference between the ask price and the bid price is the spread. For example, the bid price of stock ABC is 10.00 and the ask price is 10.10, so the difference is 10 cents and that is the spread. Ideally, if you were to place a market order to buy the stock, your order would get filled at the price of 10.10. If then you decide to sell the same stock immediately before the bid/ask prices changes, and you place a market order, your order would get filled at a price of 10.00. You have made a loss of 10 cents and the market has not changed. If your transaction was of 100 shares, the loss would total to $10 plus commissions. So, any time you place a new order, you need to factor in the cost of broker's commissions as well as the loss from bid-ask spread.

You have to be mentally prepared that the bid-ask spread is a cost you have to pay just as you should about the broker's commissions. Sometimes you may spend your time trying to find a price improvement on bid/ask price and during that time the price of the stock may changed significantly against you and this should beat the logic why you did not take what was initially offered to you.

7. Paper Trading

If you are a beginner interested in trading stocks, you most likely will welcome the idea of paper trading as it is fun to test how the stock market works. When you paper trade, you do not lose real money and the whole thing is more like a game. In paper trading, you write on paper the imagined quantity of stocks bought at the current price. You then wait for a period of time to see how the market unfolds. When the time comes when you feel you should sell your stocks, write down that price, and then all you do is to subtract the prevailing stock price for the day from the initial price you 'paid' for the stock. From this, you should be able to tell if you have made a profit or a loss for the said period. In paper trading, it's very important the buying and selling prices as well as the corresponding dates are written down on paper.

With the development of computer and internet, paper trading is today being replaced by virtual trading. Virtual trading is where you use online software, mostly free of charge, to trade imagined trades just as if it was the actual trading platform. In virtual trading, you are provided with actual prices on almost real time basis. Most stock brokers are today proving virtual trading to their customers at a small fee.

With passage of time, many paper traders will usually starts finding that the paper trading, which was initially interesting when they started, is increasingly getting boring. The reason for this feeling is because paper trading will use their time without giving them any tangible benefits or rewards. But the reward of paper trading is the trading knowledge gained without putting your money at risk. Paper trading should be done for at least six months. Alternatively, you can open a brokerage account, and whilst you trade, you can use the virtual trading platform provided by your broker to paper trade for different trading strategies that may be of interest to you.

After you are comfortable with paper trading, you may be ready to switch to actual stock trading. In actual trading, you will use your hard earned money, it's real, when you lose you lose, when you gain you gain, and that in itself makes a lot of emotions unlike in paper. Many people will get scared of actual trading but if it's done correctly, it's very rewarding. Just look around and you will notice that most of the wealthiest men and women have something to do with holding and trading shares of companies.

A day will come when your stock broker will approve your stock trading account. The next step will be for you to make your first trade. Chances are that the first trade you will make will make profit for you. And then you will get excited by that profit. That first win and the excitement that comes with it might mark the end of the party. Every time you think the market is to move upward, the market will move downwards. Every time you think the market is to move downward, the market will move upwards. And you can easily get confused and conclude the stock market doesn't work. The stock market does work for some people in-the-know who consistently make profits in every strong move of the market.

One of main difference between paper trading of stocks and actual stock trading is the emotion factors. You will realize that when it's your real money on the table, you will start watching the stock prices more frequently than never before – perhaps every hour or every five minutes. The moment prices start to move against your wishes, you will panic. This can result in you selling your stocks – and this might not be the right thing to do. The emotion factors are some of the reasons that makes people abandons their trading plans and starts trading haphazardly. This has caused many stock traders to lose huge sums of money. It is especially true for beginning stock traders.

We humans have fear and greed. Fear and greed are in most cases considered by humans as negative. You can train yourself how to overcome fear and greed. The fact that you have trained in overcoming fear and greed does not mean that if you get the direction of the stock market wrong you will not lose. What you need most is to have a trading plan based on sound know-how that takes greed and emotions as blessing in disguise. In the actual stock trading, you need to have a stock trading plan that defines when and where you are going to get out of a trade, and after you get out, what's next? That plan should include the amount of profit expected, and where to get out of the trade if the price drops beyond a defined level. Stick with your plan regardless of what the TV, newspapers and stock analysts are saying. Sooner, and your God willing, you will become a good stock trader who consistently makes profit in all the major moves of the stock market.

8. Rules of Day Trading

Day trading in the stock market is the buying and selling of the same shares or stocks on the same day. Day trading is considered too risky to inexperienced traders due to the fact that most inexperienced traders can easily get carried away by emotions. As a result, such inexperienced traders can open and close many trades in a day without paying attention to ask-bid slippage and commissions which can quickly add up into huge loses. It is because of this that small investors need protection by limiting the number of trades on the same stock that they can open and close in a single day.

The NASD and NYSE have instituted regulations to limit the number of day trades to small accounts. Any account under a net liquidation of less than, say, $25,000, is a small account and day trading rules apply. From these rules, small scale traders can only perform a maximum of three day trades within a rolling five trading-days period. This is a rule that has been approved by the Securities and Exchange Commission (SEC). The rule is called Pattern Day Trader (PDT) rule. This rule is one of the most important rules concerning day trading of stocks in US security exchanges.

Pattern Day Trading is subject to Pattern Day Trader Restrictions and as a stock trader you are penalized as follows:

1. Your stock broker is authorized to flag your account as a pattern day trader to prevent any more day trades. You may be given the option to alert your broker the rule was accidentally violated and you have no intention of becoming a day trader in which case the flagging will be removed.

2. Your account is frozen for about 3 months, or you raise you account's cash to a minimum of $25,000, whichever comes sooner.

If you can get a brokerage whose trading platform has an algorithm to prevent accounts with less than $25,000 from opening more than 3 day-trades within 5 trading days, then, the issue of being penalized from pattern day trading need not be a problem. There are some brokers out there who unfortunately will not warn you ahead of time when you are about to be flagged as a Pattern Day Trader.

It is important to note that an option exercise or assignment counts as a day trading activity. Exception is deliveries of single stock futures, lapse of options, Futures contracts and Futures Options – they are not taken as day trading activity.

8.1 Examples of Pattern Day Trades

1. You buy on Tuesday 310 shares of ABC. On the same Tuesday, towards the end of the day, you sell 350 shares of ABC. This is a day trade.

2. You buy on Wednesday 450 shares of XYZ. On the same Wednesday, towards the end of the day, you sell 500 shares of XYZ. This is a day trade.

3. You buy on Wednesday 400 shares of ABC. On the same Wednesday, during 'after hours' trading, you sell 200 shares of ABC. This is a day trade.

4. You buy on Thursday 60 shares of XYZ. On Friday morning you buy another 60 share of XYZ. On the same Friday, towards the end of the day, you sell 120 shares of XYZ. This is a day trade.

5. You buy on Friday pre-market 700 shares of ABC. On the same Friday, during 'after hours' trading, you sell 500 shares of ABC. This is a day trade.

6. You buy 5,000 December call options of XYZ 40 on Friday. On the same Friday, towards the end of the day, you sell 1,000 December call options of XYZ 40. This is a day trade

7. In a calendar spread, you buy 1,000 November call options of ABC 20 and simultaneously sell 1,000 September call options of ABC 20 on Friday. On the same Friday, towards the end of the day, you close your positions by buying 1,000 September call options of ABC 20 and simultaneously selling 1,000 November call options of ABC 20. These are 2 day trades.

What Is Not a Day Trade?

1. You buy on Tuesday 50 shares of XYZ stock. On Wednesday, you sell 50 shares of XYZ. On the same Wednesday, towards the end of the day, you buy 50 shares of XYZ stock. This is not a day trade.

2. You buy 120 shares of ABC stock on Monday and the following Tuesday you sell 300 shares of ABC stock. This is not a day trade.

That is about all there is on Rules of Day Trading. Just make sure you do not execute more than 3 day trades within 5 consecutive day's period. Else, make sure your account has at least $25,000 net liquidation all the times.

9. Exchange-Traded Funds (ETFs)

An exchange trade fund (ETF) is a security that tracks a basket of stocks or index and trade just like a stock in the stock market. ETFs fluctuate in prices during a trading day, just like stocks, as they are sold and bought. ETFs are like mutual funds only that they trade like stocks. An ETF based on an index will try to replicate that index as much as possible but sometimes the returns may deviate a bit due to volatility. ETFs are issued in 'creation units' consisting of large blocks of shares, with thousands of shares, to large investors. The large investors will then splits the 'creation units' and sells the individual shares on the secondary market. This gives the small traders an opportunity to trade on individual shares of ETFs.

1. Benefits of trading ETFs include the following:

2. They spread risks across component stocks

3. They pay dividends based on dividends paid by component stocks

4. They are less noisy in terms of volatility

5. They are not prone to rumors and, or manipulations

6. They have options, and their options are spread at workable intervals for spread strategies

7. They are easily predictable by using the broad market indices

Examples of Index based ETFs:

1. SPDR Dow Jones Industrial Average ETF (DIA)

2. Nasdaq 100 PowerShares Exchange-Traded Funds (QQQ)

3. SPDR S&P 500 (SPY)

4. iShares Russell 2000 Index Fund (IWM)

5. iShares Russell 1000 Index Fund (IWB)

III. Whipsaws in Stock Prices

1. Benefits of Whipsaws in Trading Stocks

Having learnt some of the basics about the stock market, it is now time to look at the technical aspect of trading. The aim here is to learn how one can use the benefits of whipsaws in trading stocks. People usually lose money in the stock market because they get whipsawed by the market. Whipsaws are the biggest obstacles in the stock markets. If there were no whipsaws in the stock prices, then, each one of us would be successful traders.

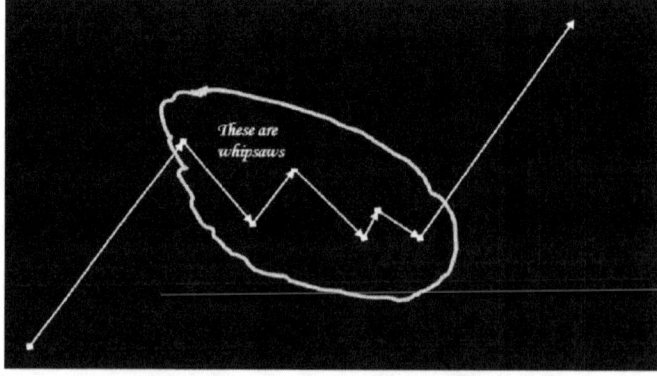

Fig. 1: An example of whipsaws

A whipsaw is a situation where a stock's price moves in one direction, and then suddenly moves in the opposite direction, as shown in the above figure. The term whipsaw is derived from whip-saws that are used by lumberjacks to cut wood. The whipsaws in stock market can continue for several weeks before finally picking on the right direction.

Whipsaws are a nuisance and will make you lose time, trading opportunities, and your trading money.

When you see two bulls fighting each other, one thing should be certain to you – that the fight will not last forever and that eventually there will be a winner and a loser. The same is also true of the stock market – the stock market can not continue whipsawing forever and that the right direction of the market will eventually be known. It is important you take note of that last statement, if you will.

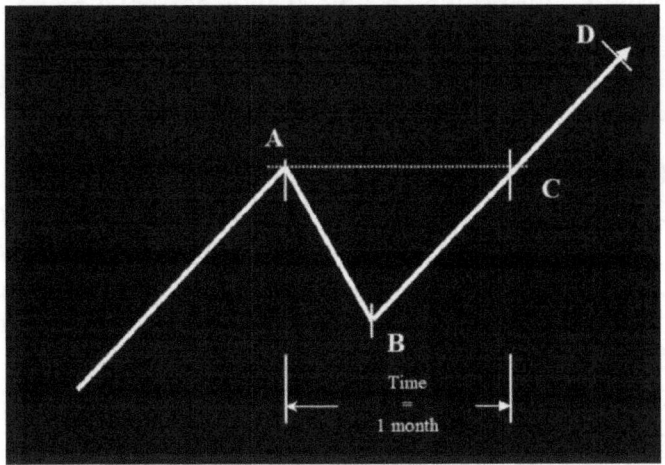

Fig 2: Whipsaws - You Lose Time, Money and Trading Opportunities

In fig 2 above, you can buy stocks at point A and hold them until the prices rise to point D. Your profit would be price D minus price A. You can also sell short the stocks at price A and buy to close at price B, then buy the stocks at price B and let the price rise to price C and again let the price rise to price D. Your profit would be price A minus price B, plus price C minus price B, and plus price D minus price C. In this case, we can conclude that if the price movement in the direction of the whipsaw is large enough, then, trading in that direction of each whipsaw will give you the following:

1. More trading opportunities

2. More profits

3. Saving in time value

A trade entered at price A will take a month to be at price C during which time it will not have made a profit. In comparison, a trade entered at price B will take about half a month to be at price C during which time it will have made a nice profit.

Unfortunately, not all price movements in the direction of whipsaws are large enough for one to make a profit trading them. In fact, most price changes in whipsaws are not large enough, and more often than not, traders make losses trying to trade them.

2. Adversity of Whipsaws

To most traders, the decision to trade is based on the expectation that the stock prices will continue in the direction of past prices. And then abruptly a whipsaw set in and the prices head in the opposite direction. To the traders, a whipsaw in stock prices is an adversity that destroys their investments.

Napoleon Hill said, "every adversity, every failure, every heartache carries with it the seed of an equal or greater benefit". If you take a whipsaw to be an adversity, then, every time you trade and encounter a whipsaw, that whipsaw is carrying with it an opportunity for you to have an equal or a greater trade.

"When God shuts one door, He opens another!" Those exact words are not in the Bible but have been borrowed from Alexander Graham Bell who said, "When one door closes another door opens, but we so often look so long and so regretfully upon the closed door, that we do not see that other door that has opened." When we trade in the direction of a stock's price and then suddenly the price moves in the opposite direction, we do find it difficult to change our minds and trade in the new direction. This is so true that even geniuses fall victim in being unable to change their minds.

In 1700, the genius Isaac Newton learnt this the hard way. Isaac Newton had invested his money in the South Sea Company. The South Sea Company was the company of the day which had the monopoly of trading African slaves for the Americans. Isaac bought shares of the company that were going for £100 and rose to £1200 per share. When the shares of that company started the downtrend, poor Isaac Newton held on to his dear shares and he lost £20,000 which was a lot of money then, and even today, £20,000 is still a lot of money. After the loss, Isaac Newton remarked that he can calculate the motions of heavenly bodies, but not the madness and emotions of people. The truth is, a stock is nothing if it's not making money to you. Throw it away to the nearest stock broker.

3. Casinos Imposes Betting Limits

Have you ever asked yourself why casinos impose betting limits for almost every single game? The main reason is because if you keep playing while raising your bet, you will never lose. And have you ever asked yourself why secure websites impose a limit on password tries of two or three guesses after which they tell you to retry latter after 24 hours? The reason is because if you keep trying, you may soon crack passwords of accounts that are not yours. This is also true in the stock market only that in the stock market there are no limits to trades – you can trade as many times as your money can allow. Unfortunately, very few traders know how to exploit this loophole in the stock market.

1. To recapitulate, let's briefly state the following:

2. Whipsaws in stock markets can not last forever

3. Every whipsaw in stock prices is a blessing in disguise

4. If you keep trading while raising your bet, you will never lose

5. A stock is nothing if it's not making money to you

6. When one trade fails, another trading opportunity presents itself with greater profits

IV. Benefits of Whipsaws in Can't Lose Trades

1. What is a Stock Trade?

A stock trade is the process of buying a stock at a lower price and holding it to sell latter at a higher price for profit. It's also the process of selling a stock short at a high price and anticipating the price to fall and buy the stock to cover the short position for a profit. A stock trade should be a process that involves several steps of buying and selling of the same stock until eventually a profit is made which is bigger than your combined losses.

In farming, we have to prepare the land, plant the seeds, do the watering, do the weeding, spray chemicals, and harvest the crop before finally selling the crop to get a profit. All these steps are part of crop management and each one of them has a cost attached to it. The same should be true when we buy stocks. We should be mentally prepared for a few more entries and exits in the same stock trades before finally making a profit. If you surrender from your stock trades after a few trading steps, then, it is like farming a crop and abandoning it altogether in the field just before the harvesting step.

2. The Only Three Things Stock Prices Can Do

In the stock market, stock prices can move up or down, at any time, and without reference to anyone.

In short, the stock prices can only do three things as follows:

1. The prices can move up in an uptrend.

2. The prices can remain neutral in a sideway move.

3. The prices can move down in a downtrend.

3. Worked Example in Can't Lose Trades

Having come this far, we are now going to look at the benefits of whipsaws in can't lose stock trades. In this worked example, we are to use an exchange traded fund (ETF) which is as good as a stock. We are to examine QQQ Power Shares, an ETF, for a period of one year in the past. QQQ shares are short-able, the shares pays dividend, and QQQ's options have well spaced strike-price intervals. QQQ is heavily traded with slim chances of large bid-ask slippages. As an ETF, QQQ is not easily manipulated since it's made up from 100 different stocks.

In this example, we are to use the end of the day price data. To identify the whipsaws we shall use the basic 10 days and 50 days moving averages, entering a trade short or long whenever the two moving averages crosses over. Latter in this document, we shall be discussing more about setting up moving averages. For now, there are two important facts to state here about moving averages. This is about the logic of counting. It's like this: From the numbers, 1,2,3,4,5,6,7,8,9,etc.,etc., we can not count number 9 before counting number 5, and we can not count number 9 before counting all those other numbers that are less than 9. That is knowledge you must have learnt in elementary education. We use this kind of logic to help identify false crossover of moving averages. It is therefore important that you make note of the following:

1. That the moving average of 10-days can not crossover the moving average of 50 days before the moving average of 5 days have crossed the moving average of 50 days. If it does cross, that is a false signal and should be ignored until the moving average of 5 days crosses over the moving average of 50 days.

2. That the moving average of 10 days can not crossover the moving average of 50 days before crossing the moving average of 30 days. If it does cross, that is a false signal and should be ignored until the moving average of 10 days crosses over the moving average of 30 days.

3. That the whole range of moving averages is a band of moving averages, and for convenient, we can only pick just a few moving averages for checking false signals. For example, when we want to use moving average of 45 days, we can pick moving averages of 30 days and 15 days to test the validity of the crossover. Others examples can be 21(14, 7), 30(20, 10), 60(40, 20), 90(60, 30), 120(80, 40), 210(140, 70), etc. The period of moving average to use is what you feel is good for you, but just make sure the two moving averages you use to confirm the validity of crossovers are appropriately

spaced at intervals of about one-third and two-thirds.

4. Very important: whichever moving average you chose to use, make sure to stick with it and to faithfully do what its telling you as if it was your deity.

The QQQ chart to this example follows:

Fig 3: QQQ Trade from October 2009 to October 2010

4. Method 1: Adding More Shares in Equal Increments after Every Loss

In this can't loss method, we add more shares in equal increments after every loss from a whipsaw until such a time we make a profit. No more, No less. In this example, we shall enter a trade long or short whenever the 10-day moving average crosses over the 50-day moving average.

1. We start with 10 shares of QQQ. We enter the trade at crossover point "A" by buying long the stock at $31. We hope the stock

price will go up. But we exit the trade at crossover point "B" by selling the stock at $29 for a loss of $2 per share. For 10 shares we make a loss of $20. Our initial investment for that trade was $310.

2. We are to trade by adding 10 more shares than we had at 1 above. So, we start this trade with 20 shares of QQQ. We enter the trade at point "B" by selling short the stock at $29. We hope the stock price will go down. We exit the trade at point "C" by buying the stock to close at $30 for a loss of $1 per share. For 20 shares we make a loss of $20. Our initial investment for that trade was, say, $290 (a short sale requires initial margin of about 50% the stock's value = 20x50%x29).

3. We are to trade by adding 10 more shares than we had at 2 above. So, we start this trade with 30 shares of QQQ. We enter the trade at point "C" by buying long the stock at $30. We hope the stock price will go up. We exit the trade at point "D" by selling the stock at $28.5 for a loss of $1.5 per share. For 30 shares we make a loss of $45. Our initial investment for that trade was $900.

4. We are to trade by adding 10 more shares than we had at 3 above. So, we start this trade with 40 shares of QQQ. We enter the trade at point "D" by selling short the stock at $28.5. We hope the stock price will go down. We exit the trade at point "E" by buying the stock to close at $30 for a loss of $1.5 per share. For 40 shares we make a loss

of $60. Our initial investment for that trade was, say, $570 (a short sale requires initial margin of about 50% the stock's value = 40x28.5x50%).

5. We are to trade by adding 10 more shares than we had at 4 above. So, we start this trade with 50 shares of QQQ. We enter the trade at point "E" by buying long the stock at $30. We hope the stock price will go up. We exit the trade at point "F", which is the end of the chart shown, by selling the stock at the price of $43. For 50 shares we make a profit of $650. Our initial investment for that trade was $1,500.

6. In the next crossover of your moving averages, you will need to start all over again as in No. 1 above since you have made a profit in No. 5.

7. Loss from No. 1 to No. 4 is: − (60 + 45+ 20+ 20) = -$145

8. Profit from No. 5 above is: = $650

9. Net profit is: 650 − 145 = $505

We have made a profit because we can't loss. But note very carefully: we started the unknown journey with $310 and ended up spending $1,500 in that last trade so that we can make that one profit of $650. This trade would have required us to have at least $1,645 (1,500+145) in the account before embarking or starting on these trades. If we did not have the courage to pull the trigger and invest $1,500 in No. 5 above after successive losses in No.1 - 4, we would have surrendered and would have lost the $145 to the market. Does this tell you anything?

If you multiplied your trades by, say, 10, you then could have made a profit of $5,050. To do such a trade, you would need to prepare your mind in advance that such a trade may end up needing $16,450, and you actually should be having that money in your account. Such money should be in cash or equity that can be liquidated for instant cash. However, if you have a margin account, your broker should be providing you with a margin (loan) of 50%. In such a case, you may just need $8,225 cash.

The whipsaws in this example were 5 since there were 5 crossovers of the moving averages. What happens if the whipsaws become more than that and there is need for more cash than you had reserved in your account? The answer to that question will be answered latter on as we proceed.

And what's happens if in this example there was only one whipsaw with only 1 crossover of the moving averages? You'd make a small profit of (43-31) x 10 = $120 without much hassle. The $120 profit from an investment of $310 may not look attractive to beginning stock traders, especially when they reflect on the fact that their stock broker is still holding idle their $8,225 cash. To solve that problem, ask your stock broker if they pay interest to idle cash in your brokerage account.

5. Method 2: Doubling Your Shares after Every Loss

In this can't loss method, we double the number of shares after every loss from a whipsaw until such a time we make a profit. No more, No less.

1. We start with 10 shares of QQQ. We enter the trade at point "A" by buying long the stock at $31. We believe the stock price is to go up. We exit the trade at point "B" by selling the stock at $29 for a loss of $2 per share. For 10 shares we make a loss of $20. Our initial investment for this trade was $310.

2. We are to trade by doubling the 10 shares we had at No. 1 above. We start this trade with 20 shares of QQQ. We enter the trade at point "B" by selling short the stock at $29. We believe the stock price is to go down. We exit the trade at point "C" by buying to close the stock at $30 for a loss of $1 per share. For 20 shares we make a loss of $20. Our initial investment for that trade was, say, 20 x 29 x 50% = $290 (a short sale requires initial margin of about 50% the stock's value).

3. We are to trade by doubling the 20 shares we had at No. 2 above. We start this trade with 40 shares of QQQ. We enter the trade at point "C" by buying long the stock at $30. We believe the stock price is to go up. We exit the trade at point "D" by selling the stock at $28.5 for a loss of $1.5 per share. For 40 shares we make a loss of $60. Our initial investment for that trade was $1,200.

4. We are to trade by doubling the 40 shares we had at No. 3 above. We start this trade with 80 shares of QQQ. We enter the trade at point "D" by selling short the stock at $28.5. We believe the stock price is to go down. We exit the trade at point "E" by buying to close the stock at $30 for a loss of $1.5 per share. For 80 shares we make a loss of $120. Our initial investment for that trade was, say, 28.5 x 80 x 50% = $1,140 (a short sale requires initial margin of about 50% the stock's value).

5. We are to trade by doubling the 80 shares we had at No. 3 above. We start this trade with 160 shares of QQQ. We enter the trade at point "E" by buying long the stock at $30. We believe the stock price is to go up. We exit the trade at point "F", which is the end of the chart shown, by selling the stock at the price of $43. For 160 shares we make a profit of (43-30) x 160 = $2,080. Our initial investment for that trade was $4,800.

6. In the next crossover of your moving averages, you will need to start all over again as in No. 1 above since you have made a profit in No. 5.

7. Loss from No. 1 to No. 4 is: − (120 + 60+ 20+ 20) = -$220

8. Profit from No. 5 above is: = $2,080

9. Net profit is: 2,080 − 220 = $1,860

We have made a profit because we can't loss. But note very carefully: we started the initial trade with

$310 and ended up spending $4800 in that last trade so that we can make that one profit of $2080. This trade would have required us to have at least $5020 (4800+220) in the account before embarking or starting on these trades. If we did not have the courage to pull the trigger and invest $4800 in No. 5 above after successive losses in No.1 - 4, we would have surrendered and would have lost the $220 to the market. Does this tell you anything? Yes, that many traders losing money in the stock market do not have the courage to go past step 1, past step 2, past step 3, past step 4, and even past step 5.

If you multiplied your trades by, say, 10, you then could have made a profit of $20,800. To do such a trade, you would need to prepare your mind in advance that such a trade may end up needing $50,200. And you actually should be having that money in your account. Such money should be in cash or equity that can be liquidated for instant cash. However, if you have a margin account, your broker should be providing you with a margin (loan) of 50%. In this case you may just need $25,200 cash.

The whipsaws in this example were 5 since there were 5 crossovers of the moving averages. What happens if the whipsaws become more than five and there is need for more cash than you had reserved in your account? The answer to that question will be answered latter on as we proceed.

And what's happens if in this example there was only one whipsaw with only 1 crossover of the moving averages? You'd make a small profit of (43-31) x 10 = $120 without much hassle. The $120 profit from an investment of $310 may not look attractive to beginning stock traders, especially when they reflect on the fact that their stock broker is still holding idle their $25,200 cash. To solve that problem, ask your stock broker if they pay interest to idle cash in your brokerage account.

By following the two methods explained above, you should be able to have an understanding of why casinos impose betting limits for almost every single game. This is because if you keep playing while raising your bet, you will never lose.

6. Best Method to Use

From the two methods, which is the best method to trade with? The answer to that question will depend mainly on two factors:

1. The experience one has in trading

2. The amount of money one has for trading

3. The period of your moving averages – longer periods have fewer whipsaws

Let's assume a trader has $5,020 cash in his brokerage margin account. With that kind of cash, the trader can comfortably do the trades in Method 2. From $5,020, the trader made a net profit of $1860

In method 1, the trader was required to have $1,645 cash in his brokerage account. From that amount, he made a net profit of $505

With $5020, the trader can do 3.05 times the trades in method 1. This would give the trader a net profit of 505 x 3.05 = $1,540. With 4 crossovers of moving averages, Method 2 had a higher profit than method 1. Method 2 had a profit of $1,860, and method 1 had a net profit of $1,540.

But suppose there was only 1 crossover and the resulting trade was a winner? A trader using method 2 would have made a net profit of (43-31) x 10 = $120. A trader with $5020 and trading using method 1 would have done 3.05 times the trades, and the net profit would have translated to 120 x 3.05 = $366. With only 1 crossover of moving averages, Method 1 had a higher profit than method 2. Method 1 had a profit of $366, and method 2 had a net profit of $120.

Naturally, method 1 would be more attractive to the less aggressive traders. However, use your ingenuity to determine the method to use.

V. Nearing A Can't Lose Stock Trade

1. Tossing a Coin

When you toss or flip a coin, there are only two possible and equally likely outcomes. You can either get a head or a tail. The chance of getting a head is 50%. The chance of getting a tail is 50%. This measure of how likely it is that an event will occur is called probability. We can therefore say that the probability of tossing a coin once and getting a head is 50%. Similarly, the probability of tossing a coin once and getting a tail is 50%.

From the same reasoning as above, when your two moving averages (M.A) make the first crossover, there are only two possible and equally likely outcomes. You can either make a profit or a loss. The chance of making a profit is 50%, and the chance of making a loss is 50%.

And by the same logic, when your two moving averages makes the second crossover, the chance of making a profit is $(0.5) + (0.5 \times 0.5) = 0.75$. When your two moving averages makes the third crossover, the chance of making a profit is $(0.5) + (0.5 \times 0.5) + (0.5 \times 0.5 \times 0.5) = 0.875$. When your two moving averages make the nth crossover, the chance of making a profit is given by the formula:

Probability = $(0.5)^1 + (0.5)^2 + (0.5)^3 \ldots \ldots (0.5)^n$

So, we can say the following about the chances of a trade wining:

1. For 1 crossover of M.A, the probability of winning = 50.0%

2. For 2 crossovers of M.A, the probability of winning = 75.0%

3. For 3 crossovers of M.A, the probability of winning = 87.5%

4. For 4 crossovers of M.A, the probability of winning = 93.8%

We can therefore conclude that as the number of whipsaws or crossovers increases, the greater the chances of getting a winning trade on the breakout of prices on either side. As we get closer to a probability of 100%, we can say, the trade is nearing a 'can't lose stock trade'.

The two tables that follow are comparing the probability of getting a winning trade and the number of whipsaws or crossovers of your two moving averages (M.A). Also shown are examples of money invested in buying shares after every crossover until the stock trade is a winner or makes a profit. Table 1 is about adding more shares in equal increments after every loss, and Table 2 is about doubling your shares after every loss.

	Crossovers	Probability	Money Invested in Buying Shares				
A	1	50.0%	300	500	1,000	2,000	5,000
B	2	75.0%	600	1,000	2,000	4,000	10,000
C	3	87.5%	900	1,500	3,000	6,000	15,000
D	4	93.8%	1,200	2,000	4,000	8,000	20,000
E	5	96.9%	1,500	2,500	5,000	10,000	25,000
F	6	98.4%	1,800	3,000	6,000	12,000	30,000
	G	H	I	J	K	L	M

Table 1: Adding More Shares in Equal Increments after Every Loss

	Crossovers	Probability	Money Invested in Buying Shares				
A	1	50.0%	300	500	1,000	2,500	5,000
B	2	75.0%	600	1,000	2,000	5,000	10,000
C	3	87.5%	1,200	2,000	4,000	10,000	20,000
D	4	93.8%	2,400	4,000	8,000	20,000	40,000
E	5	96.9%	4,800	8,000	16,000	40,000	80,000
F	6	98.4%	9,600	16,000	32,000	80,000	160,000
G	H	I	J	K	L	M	

Table 2: Doubling Your Shares after Every Loss

2. John Smith Becomes a Stock Trader

Let's take the example of John Smith who is 24 years old and has a cash of $2,500 in his margin account. Smith is interested in trading stocks of an exchange traded fund. He can trade the following ETFs: DIA, QQQ, SPY, IWM, IWB, etc. Smith has chosen to use a 42 days moving average 42(28, 14). He has picked on the moving averages of 28 and 14 to test the validity of the moving average crossovers. A moving average of 42 days is of a long enough period with fewer whipsaws than a moving average of, say, 10 days period. Smith has convinced himself to stick with the 42(28, 14) moving average and to faithfully do what it's telling him as if it was his deity.

With $2,500, Smith has a stock purchasing power of $5,000 since his brokers will automatically fund 50% of his stocks' purchases. Smith wants first to try the method of 'adding more shares in equal increments after every loss'. From table 1, smith feels the 93.8% probability of success is good enough. A probability of 93.8% is translating to 4 crossovers of the moving averages. With a stock purchasing power limit of $5,000 and a preferred success probability of 93.8%, Smith should select $4,000, position DK in Table 1. This $4,000 is the value of shares to buy at the 4th crossover of the moving averages. From Table 1, at position AK, smith will initially start by purchasing shares of $1,000 on the first crossover of moving averages. If there are no other whipsaws, then, smith will ride the $1,000 shares all the way to profit.

With a probability of 93.8%, Smith knows that his chances of wining at the 4th crossover of moving averages are very high. Naturally, it's rare to have more than 4 moving averages crossovers in the stock markets without making a breakout of prices. But it can happen. If it does happen that there are more than 4 moving averages crossovers, then, Smith will have no more spare money to add to his trades. At that point, Smith should not give up, but should use all the sale proceeds that remains after the loss in 4th crossover of moving averages to trade in the opposite direction until the breakout of prices occur in whichever direction. At the 5th crossover of moving averages, the probability of winning is 96.7%. At this point, Smith is very close to the winning trade. The biggest mistake Smith can make at this point is to give up! The rule here is: whipsaws can not last forever.

As an alternative, Smith may now want to try the second method of 'doubling his shares after every loss'. Smith has a stocks purchasing power of $5,000. Smith prefers the winning probability of 93.8%. From this, Smith should select position DJ in table 2. In this case, smith will initially start by purchasing shares of $500 on the first crossover of moving averages. If there are no other crossovers of moving averages, then, Smith will ride the $500 shares all the way to profit. Riding $500 shares to profit for method 2, should give Smith less profit than riding $1,000 shares to profit for method 1. This is one difference between method 1 and method 2.

Suppose Smith had enough cash to continue adding more shares up to the 6th crossover of moving averages in both methods. And suppose the market did make six whipsaws. In method 1, point FK, at a 98.4% probability of success, Smith would ride $6,000 shares to profit. In method 2, point FJ, at a 98.4% probability of success, Smith would ride $16,000 shares to profit. Trading $16,000 shares to profit would make a very big difference in profit as compared to trading $6,000 shares to profit. This is another difference between method 1 and method 2.

To continue doubling your shares from $500 to $16,000 in losing trades is psychologically very difficult to most people. This should explain why method 2 of doubling your shares after every loss may not be attractive to inexperienced traders. Unlike Smith, a good number of experienced and well funded traders have a good understanding of what a success probability of 98.4% means and have no problem trading using method 2.

We are all different and with varied levels of intelligence and funding. Use the data explained in the two tables here to practice using different scenarios. You should also exercise by making your own similar tables to fit different scenarios.

Out there, there are hundreds of different methods of trading in the stock market. The method you use for trading is a choice you have made out of your free will. We can not impose the method you should use for your trades.

If you have liked these methods of stock trading, and you feel you can try them, then, you should first experiment with paper trading before using your real money. You can also paper trade using the free CBOE virtual trading platform or MarketWatch's free stock market game.

3. Moving Averages

An average is the result obtained by adding different quantities together and then dividing this total by the number of quantities. It's also called the mean. For example: the average of 7, 8, and 9 is $(7+8+9)/3 = 24/3 = 8$

A moving average is an average that is recomputed for a defined data period by adding the most recent data value and dropping the oldest one. For example: the following prices were recorded each day for a period of 5 days as: 30, 31, 32, 33, and 34.

The first 3 days average will be: $(32+33+34)/3 = 33$

The second 3 days average will be: $(31+32+33)/3 = 32$

The third 3 days average will be: $(30+31+32)/3 = 31$

The results of the above, 33, 32, and 31 are the moving averages. The average 'moves' because when calculating successive values, a new value comes into the sum and an old value drops out.

There are hundreds of trading methods being used by stock traders out there. Almost every method uses a moving average in one way or the other. Yes, thousands of stock traders are using moving averages to trade the stock market in one way or the other. There are many moving averages of varying periods just as there are different types of stock traders. Moving averages are the real forces that move the markets - people's decisions to get in or out of the stock market are heavily determined by moving averages. Every trader seems to have his or her preferred moving averages. Traders' actions are determined by different moving averages and this in turn makes the movement of stock prices look like complex waves in physics.

In every trading day, the bulls and the bears are continuously pushing prices in a see-saw pivoted by moving averages. Each trader will try to take advantage of the next tops and dips. A day trader will concentrate on dynamics of day trades losing sight of the fact that at a distance are weekly traders, monthly traders, quarterly traders, yearly traders, and each trader is trying to create favorable dynamics for maximum profits based on their preferred moving averages.

4. Computation of Moving Averages

Manual computation of moving averages is a very tedious exercise. In early 20th century, stock traders used to compute moving averages manually. We are well in the 21st century and computation of moving averages should be done by a computer loaded with a statistical package. Almost every computer has MS Excel, and Excel should be sufficient to compute your moving averages as well as plotting the appropriate graphs. Computerized as you may be, you should always make sure you understand very well the logic behind what the computer is computing as well as the results given. There should be no short cuts in this.

To compute moving averages, you will need to have stock price data in your computer. Here is an exercise that you should do for yourself. Do a Google search for Yahoo finance. Go to Yahoo Finance website and download, to an excel spreadsheet, the free historical data for an ETF stock of your preference. There are many other websites that can provide free historical stock data which you can also use to download the data.

VI. How to Setup the Trading Plan in Excel

1. Moving Averages with Two Price Lines

Now that you have downloaded the historical stock data in the form of high, low and closing prices, we shall now go ahead and do an example in computing the moving averages. Most traders usually compute their moving averages using the closing prices.

The moving averages we are to compute in our example here will have a twist in the sense that they will have two price lines. One part is based on the moving averages of daily high prices for a downtrend. The second part is based on the moving averages of daily low prices for an uptrend. Our formula will be based on the following facts:

1. When the highest price of the day goes below the moving averages of the lows, we say a downtrend has started.

2. When the lowest price of the day goes above the moving averages of the highs, we say a downtrend has started.

3. We use highest high price and lowest low price for a period of say, the past 7 trading days, as a displacement separator to provide distinctive markup and markdown between the stock prices and the moving averages. This is to enable you see distinctively when the prices crosses over the moving average line. For example, in a stock chart, you may

find it difficult to tell the difference between a stock-price at, say, 31.55 and a moving average price line at, say, 31.555.

In your excel spreadsheet, you now have the historical stock prices in the form of high, low and closing prices. You have chosen the period of your moving average as, say, 48(32, 16). You could also have chosen the periods of 21(14, 7), 30(20, 10), 60(40, 20), 90(60, 30), 120(80, 40), 210(140, 70), or whatever period of moving average that is preferable to you. You have all the freedom to choose whatever period you prefer. Once you have chosen the period of your moving average, then, you have to convince your brain that the period you have chosen is the best trading period you will have to listen to. Don't listen to television, radio, newspapers, stock analysts, or friends!

Here is another exercise for you to do. Open an MS Excel worksheet and proceeds as follows:

1. Copy and paste the high of the day, low of the day, and closing of the day stock prices for a period of, say, 200 days, in column 'A', column 'B', and column 'C' respectively.

2. Insert in column 'D' the formula, "=AVERAGE(A1:A48)". Hold and drag the formula down the column as far as your data can allow.

3. Insert in column 'E' the formula, "=AVERAGE(B1:B48)". Hold and drag the formula down the column as far as your data can allow.

4. Insert in column 'F' the formula, "=MAX(A1:A7)". Hold and drag the formula down the column as far as your data can allow.

5. Insert in column 'G' the formula, "=MIN(B1:B7)". Hold and drag the formula down the column as far as your data can allow.

6. Insert in column 'H' the formula, "=IF(C1>=E1,G1,0)". Hold and drag the formula down the column as far as your data can allow.

7. Insert in column 'I' the formula, "=IF(C1<E1,F1,0)". Hold and drag the formula down the column as far as your data can allow.

8. Insert in column 'J' the formula, "=(H1+I1)". Hold and drag the formula down the column as far as your data can allow.

9. Insert in column 'K' the formula, "=IF(C1<=D1,F1,0)". Hold and drag the formula down the column as far as your data can allow.

10. Insert in column 'L' the formula, "=IF(C1>D1,G1,0)". Hold and drag the formula down the column as far as your data can allow.

11. Insert in column 'M' the formula, "=(K1+L1)". Hold and drag the formula

down the column as far as your data can allow.

12. Select the data in column 'A', say, from A1 to A120. Press and hold the Ctrl key as you select the data in column 'J', say, from J1 to J120. Select 'insert' and insert chart. Right click chart and move it to a chart location in a new sheet. Rename the chart, say, "Uptrend 48".

13. Select the data in column 'B', say, from B1 to B120. Press and hold the Ctrl key as you select the data in column 'M', say, from M1 to M120. Select 'insert' and insert chart. Right click chart and move it to a chart location in a new sheet. Rename the chart, say, "Downtrend 48".

14. On each chart, right click the X-axis, then select 'format axis', select 'scale', and then select 'categories in reverse order' so that the chart can be read from left to right. Save your work.

Drawing these charts shouldn't be difficult as they may sound. The good thing is that you will draw them once, save them, and use them for a many years. To those who have a good knowledge of Excel, it's very easy: In the first chart, you are actually drawing a chart of daily high prices and moving averages of daily low prices. On the second chart, you are actually drawing a chart of daily low prices and moving averages of daily high prices. This should take only a few minutes.

We have used QQQ data from November 3rd 2011 to April 27th 2012 in this example. You should now have two charts for 48-day moving averages as shown here:

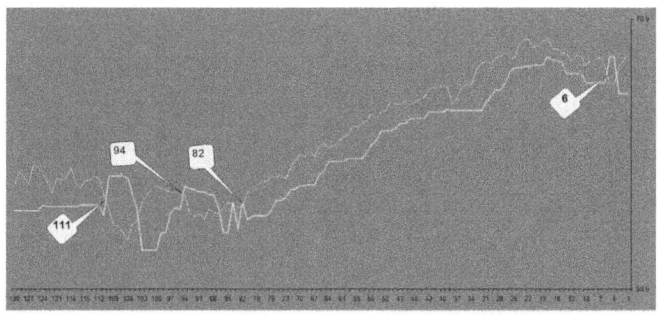

Fig 4 Uptrend chart: prices of the 48-day moving average (of lows) and prices of daily highs

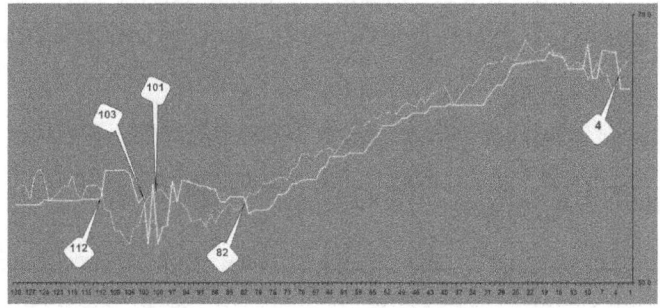

Fig 5 Downtrend chart: 48-day moving average (of highs) and prices of daily lows

Before we discuss how to make use of these charts, we'll need to make another two pairs of charts. The moving averages of 32-day and 16-day. Here is another exercise for you to do on how to make a chart for the 32-day moving averages. Open the same Excel worksheet as in the previous exercise, and proceed as follows:

1. Insert in column 'N' the formula, "=AVERAGE(A1:A32)". Hold and drag the

formula down the column as far as your data can allow.

2. Insert in column 'O' the formula, "=AVERAGE(B1:B32)". Hold and drag the formula down the column as far as your data can allow.

3. Insert in column 'P' the formula, "=MAX(A1:A7)". Hold and drag the formula down the column as far as your data can allow.

4. Insert in column 'Q' the formula, "=MIN(B1:B7)". Hold and drag the formula down the column as far as your data can allow.

5. Insert in column 'R' the formula, "=IF(C1>=O1,Q1,0)". Hold and drag the formula down the column as far as your data can allow.

6. Insert in column 'S' the formula, "=IF(C1<O1,P1,0)". Hold and drag the formula down the column as far as your data can allow.

7. Insert in column 'T' the formula, "=(R1+S1)". Hold and drag the formula down the column as far as your data can allow.

8. Insert in column 'U' the formula, "=IF(C1<=N1,P1,0)". Hold and drag the formula down the column as far as your data can allow.

9. Insert in column 'V' the formula, "=IF(C1>N1,Q1,0)". Hold and drag the formula down the column as far as your data can allow.

10. Insert in column 'W' the formula, "=(U1+V1)". Hold and drag the formula down the column as far as your data can allow.

11. Select the data in column 'A', say, from A1 to A130. Press and hold the Ctrl key as you select the data in column 'T', say, from T1 to T130. Select 'insert' and insert chart. Right click chart and move it to a chart location in a new sheet. Rename the chart, say, "Uptrend 32".

12. Select the data in column 'B', say, from B1 to B130. Press and hold the Ctrl key as you select the data in column 'W', say, from W1 to W130. Select 'insert' and insert chart. Right click chart and move it to a chart location in a new sheet. Rename the chart, say, "Downtrend 32".

13. On each chart, right click the X-axis, then select 'format axis', select 'scale', and then select 'categories in reverse order' so that the chart can be read from left to right. Save your work.

You should now have two charts for 32-day moving average as shown here:

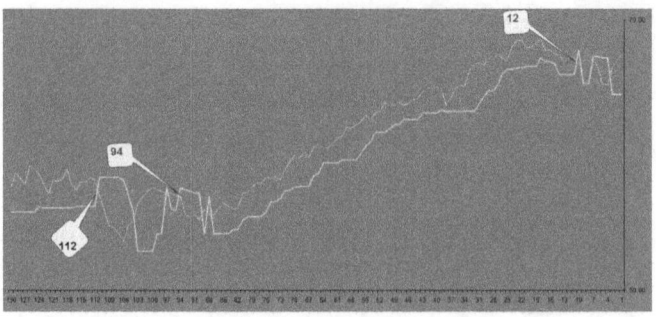

Fig 6 Uptrend chart: prices of the 32-day moving average (of lows) and prices of daily highs

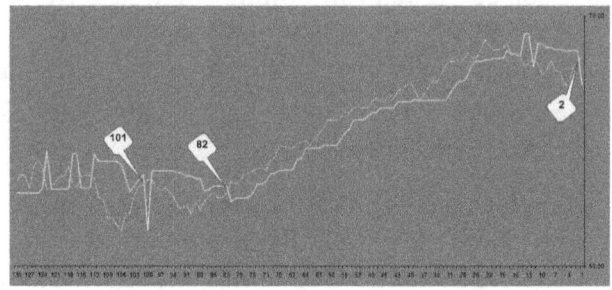

Fig 7 Downtrend chart: prices of the 32-day moving average (of highs) and prices of daily lows

Here is another exercise for you to do on how to make a chart for the 16-day moving averages. Open the same Excel worksheet as in the previous exercise, and proceed as follows:

1. Insert in column 'X' the formula, "=AVERAGE(A1:A16)". Hold and drag the formula down the column as far as your data can allow.

2. Insert in column 'Y' the formula, "=AVERAGE(B1:B16)". Hold and drag the

formula down the column as far as your data can allow.

3. Insert in column 'Z' the formula, "=MAX(A1:A7)". Hold and drag the formula down the column as far as your data can allow.

4. Insert in column 'AA' the formula, "=MIN(B1:B7)". Hold and drag the formula down the column as far as your data can allow.

5. Insert in column 'AB' the formula, "=IF(C1>=Y1,AA1,0)". Hold and drag the formula down the column as far as your data can allow.

6. Insert in column 'AC' the formula, "=IF(C1<Y1,Z1,0)". Hold and drag the formula down the column as far as your data can allow.

7. Insert in column 'AD' the formula, "=AB1+AC1". Hold and drag the formula down the column as far as your data can allow.

8. Insert in column 'AE' the formula, "=IF(C1<=X1,Z1,0)". Hold and drag the formula down the column as far as your data can allow.

9. Insert in column 'AF' the formula, "=IF(C1>X1,AA1,0)". Hold and drag the formula down the column as far as your data can allow.

10. Insert in column 'AG' the formula, "=AE1+AF1)". Hold and drag the formula down the column as far as your data can allow.

11. Select the data in column 'A', say, from A1 to A130. Press and hold the Ctrl key as you select the data in column 'AD', say, from AD1 to AD130. Select 'insert' and insert chart. Right click chart and move it to a chart location in a new sheet. Rename the chart, say, "Uptrend 32".

12. Select the data in column 'B', say, from B1 to B130. Press and hold the Ctrl key as you select the data in column 'AG', say, from AG1 to AG130. Select 'insert' and insert chart. Right click chart and move it to a chart location in a new sheet. Rename the chart, say, "Downtrend 32".

13. On each chart, right click the X-axis, then select 'format axis', select 'scale', and then select 'categories in reverse order' so that the chart can be read from left to right. Save your work.

You should now have two charts for 16-day moving average as shown here:

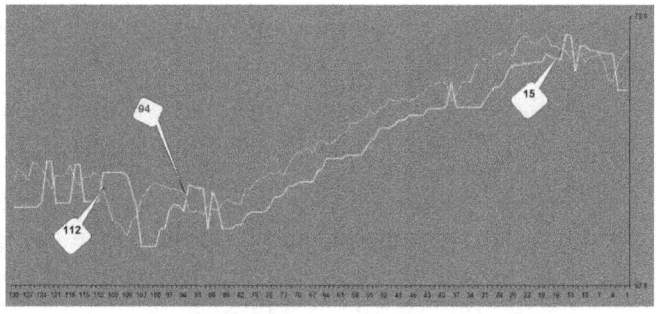

Fig 8 Uptrend chart: prices of the 16-day moving average (of lows) and prices of daily highs

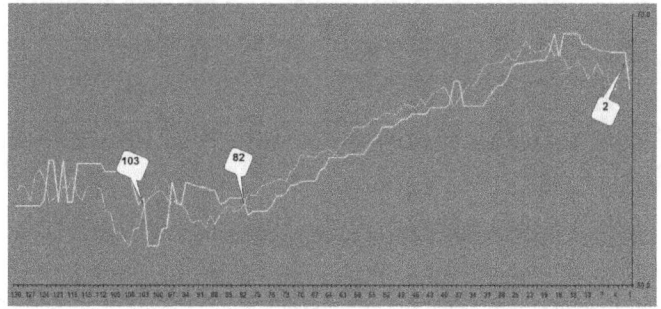

Fig 9 Downtrend chart: prices of the 16-day moving average (of highs) and prices of daily lows

2. Interpreting the Charts

We now have the six charts. It's very easy to set and interpret them since we are using a computer. Let's now look at how to trade using the three pairs of charts. You will start with Fig 4 Uptrend chart - prices of the 48-day moving average (of lows) and prices of daily highs. From point 130 to point 111, the prices of daily highs are above the 48-day moving average of daily lows. This is an uptrend. At point 111, prices of daily highs moves below the 48-day moving average of daily lows. This must be confirmed by the lower moving averages of 32-day and 16-day, otherwise, you have a false signal and the trading trend should remain uptrend. You confirm this developing downtrend as follows:

1. Fig 8 Uptrend chart: Have the prices of daily highs moved below the 16-day moving average of daily lows. The answer should be "yes"; otherwise it's a false signal.

2. Fig 6 Uptrend chart: Have the prices of daily highs moved below the 32-day moving average of daily lows. The answer should be "yes"; otherwise it's a false signal.

In this case, it was not until point 112 that the downtrend was confirmed as shown in fig 6 and fig 8.

Having confirmed the downtrend above, you move to Fig 5 Downtrend chart – 48-day moving average (of highs) and prices of daily lows. From point 112 to point 103, the prices of daily lows are below the 48-day moving average of daily highs. This is a downtrend. At point 103, prices of daily lows moves above the 48-day moving average of daily highs. This must be confirmed by the lower moving averages of 32-day and 16-day, otherwise, you have a false signal and the trading trend should remain downtrend. You confirm this developing uptrend as follows:

1. Fig 9 Downtrend chart: Have the prices of daily lows moved above the 16-day moving average of daily highs? The answer should be "yes"; otherwise it's a false signal.

2. Fig 7 Downtrend chart: Have the prices of daily lows moved above the 32-day moving average of daily highs? The answer should be "yes"; otherwise it's a false signal.

In this case, it was not until point 101 for fig 7 (and point 103 for fig 9) that the uptrend was confirmed as shown in fig 7 and fig 9.

Now that you have confirmed the uptrend at point 101 above, you will next move to Fig 4 Uptrend chart - prices of the 48-day moving average (of lows) and prices of daily highs. From point 101 to point 94, the prices of daily highs are above the 48-day moving average of daily lows. This is an uptrend. At point 94, prices of daily highs moves below the 48-day moving average of daily lows. This must be confirmed by the lower moving averages of 32-day and 16-day, otherwise, you have a false signal and the trading trend should remain uptrend. You confirm this developing downtrend as follows:

1. Fig 8 Uptrend chart: Have the prices of daily highs moved below the 16-day moving average of daily lows. The answer should be "yes"; otherwise it's a false signal.

2. Fig 6 Uptrend chart: Have the prices of daily highs moved below the 32-day moving average of daily lows. The answer should be "yes"; otherwise it's a false signal.

In this case, it was not until point 94 that the downtrend was confirmed as shown in fig 6 and fig 8.

Having confirmed the downtrend above, you move to Fig 5 Downtrend chart – 48-day moving average (of highs) and prices of daily lows. From point 94 to point 82, the prices of daily lows are below the 48-day moving average of daily highs. This is a downtrend. At point 82, prices of daily lows moves above the 48-day moving average of daily highs. This must be confirmed by the lower moving averages of 32-day and 16-day, otherwise, you have a false signal and the trading trend should remain downtrend. You confirm this developing uptrend as follows:

1. Fig 9 Downtrend chart: Have the prices of daily lows moved above the 16-day moving average of daily highs? The answer should be "yes"; otherwise it's a false signal.

2. Fig 7 Downtrend chart: Have the prices of daily lows moved above the 32-day moving average of daily highs? The answer should be "yes"; otherwise it's a false signal.

In this case, it was not until point 82 for fig 7 (and point 82 for fig 9) that the uptrend was confirmed as shown in fig 7 and fig 9.

After you have confirmed the uptrend, you move to Fig 4 Uptrend chart - prices of the 48-day moving average (of lows) and prices of daily highs. As you can see, the whipsaws ended at point 82. What follows next is a breakout of prices that you ride on up to point 6. If you added your shares accordingly after every loss in the previous whipsaws, its now time for you to make huge profits that will take care of the loss that you may have had in the previous whipsaws. Stick with fig 4 uptrend chart from point

82 up to point 6. During that time you don't need to bother with the other 5 charts. Now that you have made a profit, then, the trades end at point 6. After point 6, you will start with news trades all over again.

These trades are tabulated here. Notice that in the second row, the whipsaw of November 16th to December 2nd made a small profit. It is because of that profit that we had to start the trades all over again in the 2nd crossover of moving averages. If we had used a longer period of moving averages, that whipsaw that brought that profit may have given us a loss, and in the final analysis, a far much bigger profit than we got here. In this case, we are starting with 100 shares of QQQ and increasing the shares by 100 shares after every loss from a whipsaw. What is shown as negative shares means the shares were sold short.

The statement, 'if we had used a longer period of moving averages', is wishful thinking and you should not be tempted to fall into that trap. Just stick to your chosen period of moving average!

Train yourself to draw tables like the one shown here whenever you do these types of trades.

QQQ Shares	Entry Date	Entry Price	Exit Date	Exit Price	Profit
-100	11.16.2011	57.17	12.02.2011	56.62	55.00
100	12.02.2012	56.62	12.13.2011	55.76	-86.00
-200	12.13.2012	55.76	12.30.2011	55.83	-14.00
300	12.30.2012	55.83	04.20.2012	65.68	2955.00
				Total Profit	2855.00

Table 3: Adding More Shares in Equal Increments after Every Loss

Well, that's it. A profit of $2,855 may not look like a lot of money for a period of five months. But it is. It is a lot of money when you consider that you have a multiplier which is unlikely to get saturated with the amount of money you pump in to it – the stock market will just go ahead and multiply the profits you make again and again.

The key to success in this method of trading will depend on the discipline you have in following your chosen moving average. Choose the period of your moving average wisely and stick with it. Convince yourself that your chosen period of moving average is the best there is so that you can believe in it. This sounds easy but it's the hardest part, especially to those who are more educated. The moment you start asking yourself why are you using the moving average of say, 30, and not the moving average of say, 40, then, you will have a lot of problem in making trading decisions to benefit from these methods of nearing to a can't lose trade. You will need to use your brain to lie to the same brain that your chosen period of moving averages is the best in the industry.

As an example, and at the risk of sounding superstitious, a trader by the name John Smith can say that there are 252 trading days in a year. In every quarter, companies do report their earnings as well as pays dividends. A quarter of a year is 252/4 = 63 days. Smith can therefore lie to his brain that the best period of his moving average is 63 days. Smith can use the corresponding thirds to get periods of 21 days and 42 days for confirming the change of trend. Alternatively, if Smith is an expert in Excel, he can modify his program in Excel so that he can use the entire band of moving averages from a period of 2 days to 62 days to confirm the crossover of his 63-day moving average.

Another trader can convince himself to use a period of 72 just because he was born in 1972. Another trader may argue that people are paid their salaries at the end of every month and that a period of 24 days is good for him because there are 24 trading days in a month. Another large trader by the name Janet feels that a longer period has fewer whipsaws than a shorter period, and she pick for herself a period of 200 just because she believes that the 200-day moving average is the most popular average with traders. Pick any period that is right for you and above all, use your ingenuity and follow strictly what your moving average is telling you. Write that number next to your bed and if possible write it on the ceiling to your bedroom so that you can see it everyday. That number is everything as far as the trading of the stock market is concerned. If you tell people about your number they may start thinking all is not well with you. So, keep it as a secret because it is only you who knows what it means.

Rather than panic because a whipsaw is about to form, you should instead look forward to a whipsaw forming because it will give you an opportunity to make more profit. Just like there is no money that is too much, the opposite is also true – there is no money that is too little. Even if you only have a spare of $1000 to trade, plan your little money as explained in the methods of this document and you will be able to teach whipsaws a lesson in your own small way. Like a smart soldier, always make sure that before you shoot, you have sufficient spare bullets.

3. Exercises

(i) Great Depression Aug 1929 – Mar 1933

You may not have been born in 1929. It was on October 29, 1929 that the stock market plunged heavily. They called that day, "Black Tuesday". The Black Tuesday symbolizes the start of the Great Depression. What followed was a crush of the stock markets worldwide. The banking system collapsed. There was an extremely deep depression. To many traders in the stock market, it was the end of the world.

Get the Dow Jones Industrial Average data for the period August 1929 to March 1933 from Yahoo Finance. Using the knowledge gained from this document, analyze that data using your chosen moving average to get the feel and see if you could have made a profit then.

You should assume one unit of DJI to be one share and take the entry or exit price as the day closing price of the index. You will use the index prices because the data for stocks may not be available for that period or that most of the companies that traded in those days no longer exists today.

(ii) As in (i) above, analysis the Dow Jones Industrial average data for the following recession periods:

1. 1937 Recession from May 1937 to June 1938

2. 1945 Recession from February 1945 to October 1945

3. 1949 Recession from November 1948 to October 1949

4. 1953 Recession from July 1953 to May 1954

5. 1958 Recession from August 1957 to April 1958

6. 1960 Recession from April 1960 to February 1961

7. 1969 Recession from December 1969 to November 1970

(iii) Get the NASDAQ Composite data for the period February 1971 to March 1999 from Yahoo Finance. As in (ii) above, analysis the NASDAQ Composite average data for the following recession periods:

1. 1973 Recession from November 1973 to March 1975

2. 1980 recession from January 1980 to November 1982

3. 1982 Great Bull Market from 1982 to 2000

(iv) Get from Yahoo Finance the QQQ data for the period January 2000 to December 2011. As in number (iii) above, analysis the QQQ data for the entire period - January 2000 to December 2011

Postscript

What you have learnt in this document has been drawn from many years of experience trading in the stock market. Take this opportunity to make better use of this knowledge to improve your trading in stocks. It's only fair that each one of us, regardless of one's status, is entitled to a piece of the stock market's cake. If you diligently put the knowledge explained here to use by following the procedures, you will not get it wrong.

The work that lies ahead of you is a lot but will get smaller and smaller each day after you make that first step. And eventually a day will come when you will find you have made your first profitable trade, but that will only be the beginning. Certainly, your hard work should bring you many excellent trades.

If you would like to share this document with relatives, friends and associates, you should encourage them to buy additional copies for themselves, or you can purchase an additional copy for each person as a gift.